BATMAN RETURNS™
ONE DARK CHRISTMAS EVE

THE ILLUSTRATED HOLIDAY CLASSIC

WRITTEN BY IVAN COHEN

ILLUSTRATED BY JJ HARRISON

BASED ON
SCREENPLAY BY DANIEL WATERS
STORY BY DANIEL WATERS AND SAM HAMM

BATMAN CREATED BY BOB KANE WITH BILL FINGER

INSIGHT
EDITIONS

SAN RAFAEL · LOS ANGELES · LONDON

Their son was not a worthy heir,
"He's sure no prince," they seethed.
So they tossed him out like a week-old fish.
They were selfish!
Revenge would be that child's fav'rite dish.

Now Gotham City's mayor rings in
Its unique Christmastime—
A winter wonderland despite
The violence and crime.

Along with retail king Max Shreck
Who smiles out on the square,
So naïve about what lies in store.
They can't ignore
A present they will soon come to abhor!

They kidnap Max, and then attack
His aide, Selina Kyle.
The cops, sure they'd lose the brutal fight,
Shine a bright light
In the sky to summon the Dark Knight!

To meet the lord of Gotham's lost,
Who needs a hand from Max.
United, they are destined to win—
Commit ev'ry sin!—
Max Shreck and his partner, The Penguin!

Selina goes to Shreck's office
After business hours.
Finds plans to rob the city blind
And give Max all the power.

When he returns and finds her there,
He shoves her to her death,
Confident that he'd never be caught—

That's what he thought—
But Catwoman is what he really wrought!

The gang now follows Max's scheme
Committing crimes nonstop.
And thwarting all their heinous deeds:

The Penguin, not the cops!
The public eats it with a spoon,
And in no time at all,

The Penguin is the king of Gotham fair—
Running for mayor!—
He's claimed his name and
now Batman beware!

Bruce Wayne suspects that something's wrong
With Max and Oswald's deal.
Distracted by Selina's charms,
He asks her to a meal.

But first they have another date,
With masks and with a whip.
The Cat says mistletoe's a poison thing—

Foreshadowing!—
Oh vengeance interferes with romancing!

At Wayne Manor Bruce attempts to woo
Quirky Selina Kyle.
They're broken in such similar ways,

They make each other smile.
But news of a kidnapping means
They both must cut things short.

OH, I UH, HAVE A **BIG** BUSINESS DEAL TO UH...

OH SH-- UM, LOOK AT THE TIME.

WE REPEAT: THE ICE PRINCESS HAS BEEN **KIDNAPPED!**

For each one knows that crime is still job one—
No time for fun
With an Ice Princess's life so close to done!

Batman's too late to stop her fall,
She never had a chance!
What's more, the gang has rigged the scene,
Now Gotham looks askance,
As Batman's guilt seems ironclad
With bats filling the air.

His car hijacked, a bad night gets much worse—
Is this the last verse?—
The Batmobile may become a hearse!

The Penguin steers the Batmobile,
Cackling with fiendish glee,
As Batman strives to regain control
And save Gotham City!

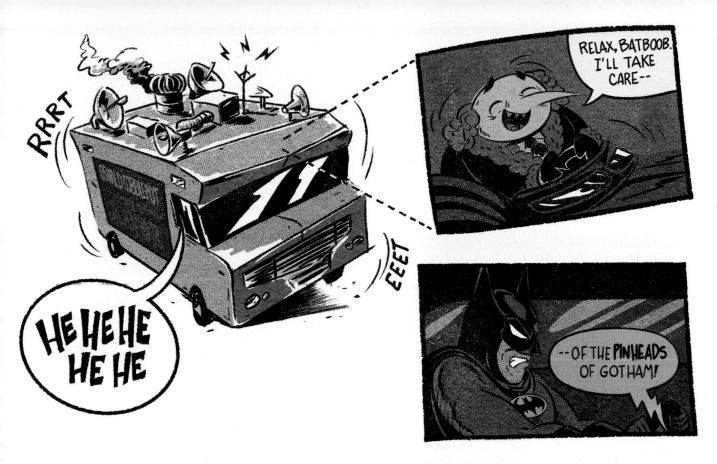

The mastermind reveals his plan
While Batman finds a way!
Breaking through the floor, why, that's the key—
Voids warranty!—
From Gotham City's Finest he must flee!

The mayor's race seems in the bag,
The Penguin's victory sealed.
"His Honor Cobblepot" sounds good,
Is how the voters feel.

But Batman has his hateful words
Recorded on a disk.
And when The Penguin's true contempt is shown,
Tomatoes are thrown!
Dreams of power he must surely disown.

When The Penguin kidnaps Max
he steals the show!

With his former ally in a cage
Oswald takes deadly aim.
His missile-loaded penguins will,
On Gotham City, rain
Mayhem and fire and terror like
No one has ever seen.

Those birds can't fly, but one hero can—
Hey it's Batman!
In the Batplane, foiling The Penguin's plan!

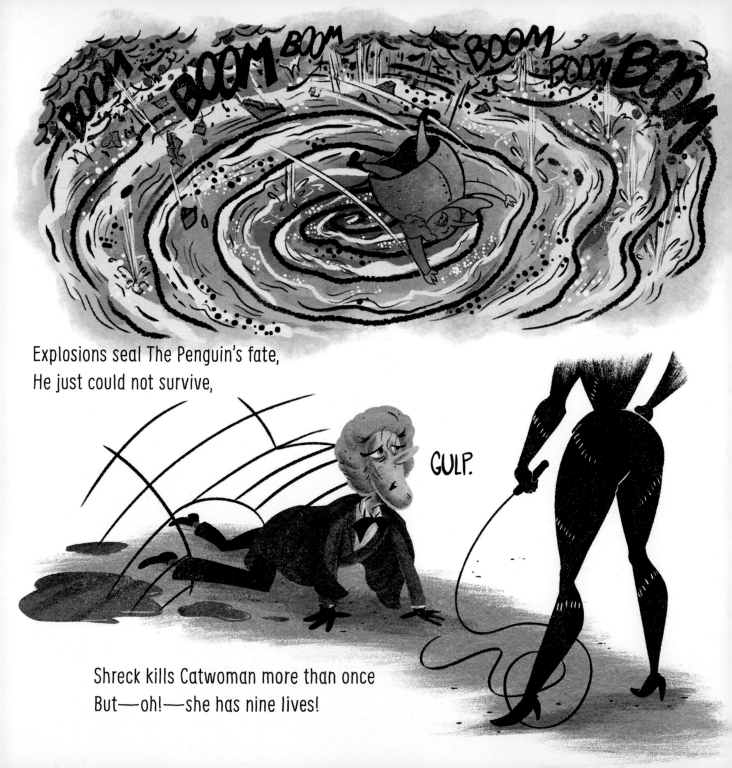

Explosions seal The Penguin's fate,
He just could not survive,

Shreck kills Catwoman more than once
But—oh!—she has nine lives!

She'll take revenge on Max despite
The Batman's heartfelt pleas.
Unmasked, Bruce asks Selina to relent;

But mercy's spent—
And to a shocking death Max Shreck is sent!

The streets of Gotham, calm at last,
With Max and Oswald dead.

But Batman finds no trace of she
Who had so turned his head.

Did Catwoman somehow endure?
Bruce and Alfred cannot tell.

A stray cat's the only feline in sight—
Hope still shines bright!

Merry Christmas,
    and to all a Dark Knight!